THE
TURMERIC
COOKBOOK

An Hachette UK Company
www.hachette.co.uk

First published in Great Britain in 2017 by Aster, an imprint of
Octopus Publishing Group Ltd, Carmelite House,
50 Victoria Embankment, London EC4Y 0DZ
www.octopusbooks.co.uk

Distributed in the US by Hachette Book Group, 1290 Avenue of the
Americas, 4th and 5th Floors, New York, NY 10104

Distributed in Canada by Canadian Manda Group, 664 Annette St.,
Toronto, Ontario, Canada M6S 2C8

ISBN 978-1-91202-311-0

Printed and bound in China.

10 9 8 7 6 5 4 3

Consultant Publisher Kate Adams
Recipe Developer and Food Stylist Nicole Pisani, Food for Happiness
Additional Recipes Oliver Pagani
Cocktail Recipes Gosia Zielony
Senior Designer Jaz Bahra
Senior Editor Leanne Bryan
Copy Editor Clare Sayer
Photographer Issy Croker
Props Stylist Emily Ezekiel
Production Manager Caroline Alberti

Page 7 picture credit: Wellcome Library, London

THE
TURMERIC
COOKBOOK

Discover the health benefits
and uses of turmeric, with
50 delicious recipes

CONTENTS

INTRODUCTION

Turmeric, the spice best known as an ingredient in curries, is one of nature's most powerful ancient healers and has been used medicinally for more than 4,500 years. It comes from the root of *Curcuma longa*, a green plant in the ginger family, and is grown throughout the tropics, especially in India and Indonesia. On the island of Bali, turmeric is at the heart of their traditional medicine and "jamu" tonics are widely available to cure ailments and boost well-being.

Turmeric appears in some of the earliest known records of plant medicines. It is mentioned in Ancient Egyptian texts and is thought to have been cultivated in the Gardens of Babylon, one of the Seven Wonders of the Ancient World. In India, turmeric has played an important part in Ayurvedic medicine for 2,500 years. Inhaling the fumes from burning turmeric was said to alleviate congestion; turmeric paste or juice was used to heal wounds and bruises; and the spice was also used for digestive issues.

Modern medicine is now beginning to confirm many of the reported health benefits of turmeric and especially its anticancer properties. Much of the research is focused on one of the main components of turmeric, a substance called curcumin. However, attention is now also being directed at studying the effects of the whole root, and the pages that follow will explore all the potential health benefits of this wonder root.

COOKING WITH TURMERIC

We are all starting to hear more about turmeric and how it might be a good idea to include plenty of it in our diets. But beyond curry, how do we do that?

As it happens, alongside the increased attention of the medical community, chefs and healthy foodies have been trying out turmeric in an amazing array of dishes. Traditional "golden milks" and tonics are growing in popularity; turmeric teas and turmeric honey are now available; and supermarkets are beginning to sell fresh turmeric root alongside fresh ginger root, as well as ground or powdered turmeric.

Turmeric has a very individual taste that is hard to describe, except to say it is quite pungent and bitter. However, when combined with other ingredients its culinary use widens considerably. For example it goes well with honey and so can be used in desserts, on top of porridge, or in granola. You can use it in baked goods, on roasted vegetables, in salad dressings, or even in ice cream.

Turmeric has antiaging properties, so it can also be used as a natural beauty ingredient. In this book we've included some different face masks to try along with a turmeric body scrub.

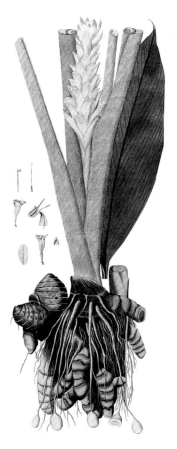

> "Each spice has a special day to it. For turmeric it is Sunday, when light drips fat and butter-colored into the bins to be soaked up glowing, when you pray to the nine planets for love and luck."
> — Chitra Banerjee Divakaruni, *The Mistress of Spices*

ANCIENT HEALER, MODERN MEDICINE

While the Assyrians and the Ancient Greeks knew about and used turmeric, it was Asian herbalists—likely due to turmeric needing tropical conditions to thrive—who made the most medicinal use of this spice. Europeans only began to catch on to the idea of using turmeric in the late 20th century.

In Ayurveda (the Indian system of herbal medicine previously mentioned), turmeric is thought to "strengthen and warm" the system. It is used specifically to aid the digestive system and microbiome, regulate menstruation, relieve arthritic inflammation, and balance the metabolism. It is also used as an anti-inflammatory and antibacterial agent for coughs and colds and on the skin for burns, cuts, and bruises.

The Ancient Hawaiians were also thought to use turmeric for conditions including ear and sinus infections, most probably due to its astringent properties. And across Indonesia, the recipes for turmeric tonics are still closely guarded family secrets, used in the traditional herbal healing system known as 'Jamu', both for general preventive well-being and for the treatment of specific conditions, such as joint pain.

In Europe, serious research on the health properties of turmeric began in Germany in the 1920s, and in the 1960s its benefits to the digestive system started to be discussed. By the 1990s, turmeric was more regularly recommended by western herbalists and today doctors and general practitioners often recommend turmeric as part of a healthy diet, especially for cancer patients.

Research into the heart-health benefits of turmeric has focused on curcumin, its main active ingredient. This has been shown to have anti-inflammatory effects, and it is also an antioxidant. Inflammation has been linked to heart disease, diabetes, Alzheimer's, stroke, and cancer. Antioxidants protect the body from the damage caused by free radicals, which we are exposed to through normal bodily processes such as burning sugars for energy or digestion, and through our environment. The anti-inflammatory and antioxidant effects of turmeric are also linked to benefitting overall health and well-being when included in a healthy diet.

Recently, studies have shown the potential anticancer benefits of turmeric, specifically when consumed through cooking. It is thought that it may be helpful both as part of a preventive lifestyle and for cancer patients undergoing treatment.

DOSAGE

It is currently thought that about a teaspoon of fresh or ground turmeric a day is helpful for promoting gut health and general wellbeing.

TURMERIC AND BLACK PEPPER

Black pepper contains the compound piperine that helps increase absorption of curcumin. It isn't necessary to always consume turmeric with black pepper, but it has been shown to boost the body's ability to absorb the beneficial properties.

PREPARATION AND USES

The ground turmeric that we easily recognize from its bright orange color comes from the fingers that grow from the root. The root is cleaned, boiled, and then dried at a low temperature before being processed into a powder. Fresh turmeric can also be used in a similar way to fresh ginger root, grated directly into recipes or infused in oils or in hot water for tea (see page 114). Turmeric root, which is now more readily available in supermarkets and delis, has a slightly sweeter taste than the powder.

Turmeric can be eaten both raw and cooked. For example you can grate it into dressings, ice cream, or tonics (see pages 37, 104, and 111), or add a little to soups and stews (see pages 42, 47, and 52).

WHEN EVERYTHING TURNS YELLOW

The only problem with turmeric is that it can easily discolor your pots and pans, your worktops and even your hands and fingernails. Lemon juice or white vinegar can remove the coloring, or for more stubborn stains you can use a bleach-based cleaner. If you spill a little sauce that has turmeric in it, you can try sprinkling it with talcum powder or baking soda and then blot gently with paper towels. The key is to try not to rub it in. For clothing, sometimes bleach is the only answer, but apparently soaking the item and putting it in sunlight may help to fade the stain. And for your skin, try mixing sugar and water and gently scrubbing your hands; this works as a natural exfoliator at the same time as removing that lovely yellow hue.

BREAKFASTS

BIRCHER MUESLI
WITH TURMERIC HONEY

Soaking oats overnight makes breakfast quick and easy in the morning. You can then simply heat them up with a little extra milk or water and serve with a spoonful of turmeric honey, or turn it into a Bircher muesli with some chopped fruit and nuts.

1 cup rolled oats

1 tablespoon flaxseeds

1 tablespoon chia seeds

¼ teaspoon ground cinnamon

½ cup unsweetened almond milk

1 cup water

few drops of vanilla extract

2 apples

juice of ½ lime

2 tablespoons natural yogurt

1 tablespoon hazelnuts, coarsely
    chopped

2 tablespoons turmeric honey
    (see below)

1 teaspoon coconut oil (optional)

To serve (optional)

Spiced and Roasted Seeds
    (see page 30)

Thai basil leaves (optional)

**For the turmeric honey
    (makes ¾ cup)**

3 tablespoons coconut oil

½ cup raw liquid honey

2 teaspoons ground turmeric

¼ teaspoon ground black pepper

First make the turmeric honey. Heat the coconut oil so that it is in liquid form. Add to a bowl with the honey, turmeric, and pepper and stir to combine thoroughly. Transfer to a glass jar, seal securely, and store at room temperature until needed.

The night before, mix together the oats, seeds, cinnamon, almond milk, water, and vanilla extract in a large bowl and let chill in the refrigerator overnight.

In the morning, grate 1 of the apples into the oats. Then stir in the lime juice, yogurt, chopped hazelnuts, and turmeric honey until combined.

Slice the remaining apple and, if liked, sauté the slices in coconut oil. Set them on top of the Bircher muesli, then finish by scattering the muesli with spiced and roasted seeds and a few Thai basil leaves (if using).

◇◇◇◇◇◇

COCONUT AND CASHEW GRANOLA

Making your own granola means you can add all your favorite things.
The coconut flakes and cashews used here create a light granola while the
honey and cinnamon add just the right amount of sweetness.

2¼ cups jumbo oats

¾ raw cashews, coarsely chopped

½ cup pumpkin seeds

½ cup sunflower seeds

2½ tablespoons golden flaxseeds

½ teaspoon ground cinnamon

½ teaspoon ground turmeric

½ teaspoon ground ginger

2 heaped tablespoons coconut oil

3 tablespoons raw liquid honey

1 teaspoon vanilla extract

Preheat the oven to 275°F and line a large baking pan with parchment paper.

Mix all the dry ingredients together in a large bowl.

Heat the coconut oil and honey in a saucepan until dissolved, then add the vanilla extract. Pour this into the dry ingredients and stir to coat the oats, nuts, and seeds thoroughly.

Pour the granola onto the paper and spread out in an even layer. Bake for about 1 hour until golden and just crunchy. Turn the oven off and let the granola cool inside the oven. Then gently bring up the sides of the paper to transfer the granola to an airtight jar.

DEVILED SCRAMBLED EGGS
WITH AVOCADO ON TOAST

Adding a few spices to your eggs makes the perfect
accompaniment to avocado on toast. This dish is
great for a Sunday brunch.

4 eggs

½ teaspoon ground turmeric

¼ teaspoon hot paprika

¼ teaspoon chili powder

⅓ cup milk (or nondairy alternative)

2 thick slices of sourdough bread

extra virgin olive oil, for drizzling

1 ripe avocado

juice of ½ lemon

2 teaspoons butter or coconut oil

good pinch of dried red chile flakes

sea salt flakes

Crack the eggs into bowl and beat with the spices
and milk.

Preheat the broiler. Drizzle the sourdough slices with
extra virgin olive oil, sprinkle with sea salt flakes, and
place under the broiler.

Meanwhile, cut the avocado in half and remove the
seed. Scoop out the flesh and mash it with the lemon
juice and a little salt.

Melt the butter or coconut oil in a nonstick skillet over
high heat and crack in the eggs along with a good pinch
of salt. Let cook for several seconds until it starts to set
on the bottom and then gently fold the eggs over and
into one another. Do not stir the eggs. Remove from the
heat when the mixture is still just slightly liquid.

Spread the toasted sourdough with the mashed avocado
and spoon the scrambled eggs on top. Sprinkle with the
chile flakes and serve immediately.

FRITTATA

The best method for getting anyone to eat more green vegetabless is to find a way to combine them with eggs and cheese. This frittata is simple but the trick is to get the heat high enough that the eggs puff up when they hit the pan, similar to an omelet.

1 tablespoon coconut oil
1 teaspoon grated fresh
    ginger root
1 teaspoon grated fresh turmeric
7oz cavolo nero (black kale),
    stalks removed and leaves
    coarsely chopped
4 large eggs
walnut-sized lump of butter
1 tablespoon crème fraîche
    (or sour cream)
3½oz sheep milk cheese, shaved
sea salt and ground black pepper

Preheat the oven to 425°F.

Heat the coconut oil in a small, nonstick, ovenproof skillet. Add the ginger and turmeric and fry over medium heat until you can smell the aroma. Add the cavolo nero, season with salt and pepper, and let it wilt in the heat. Remove from the heat, transfer to a bowl, and massage the wilted leaves with your hands.

Beat the eggs vigorously while you melt the butter in the same pan over high heat. Stir the crème fraîche (or sour cream) into the eggs and, once the skillet is very hot and the butter is foaming, add the egg mixture. The edges should puff up immediately. Add shavings of cheese and the wilted greens before transferring the pan to the oven. Cook for about 5 minutes, until the top is puffed up and golden. Serve immediately.

SMOKED MACKEREL TURMERIC CONGEE

Congee is simply rice that has been cooked longer that usual so that it gets very soft. It's similar to risotto but comes from Asia and is often eaten for breakfast as a kind of savory porridge.

2 tablespoons sesame oil

thumb-sized piece of fresh ginger root, peeled and thinly sliced

3 garlic cloves, thinly sliced

1 teaspoon ground turmeric

1 cup short-grain rice, washed thoroughly

4 dried shiitake mushrooms, rehydrated in warm water

2 cups chicken or fish stock

2 cups water

¼ cup light soy sauce

To serve

2 eggs

1 tablespoon vinegar, for poaching

2 large smoked mackerel fillets, at room temperature

1 shallot, thinly sliced

1 radish, thinly sliced

few sprigs of lemon verbena (or use picked cilantro leaves)

Heat 1 tablespoon of the sesame oil in a saucepan over medium heat and lightly fry the ginger and garlic. You don't want much color so fry them until they're aromatic and just slightly softer. Add the turmeric and stir well.

Add the rice and the shiitake mushrooms to the pan and mix everything through thoroughly. (The mushrooms are included to add a little background umami to the flavor of the dish.)

Add the stock and the water and cook over a low heat for about 1 hour, or until the rice becomes soft and similar to porridge in texture with a fair amount of liquid left in the pan. If the congee gets too dry just add some more water or stock until the consistency has returned. Once the rice is cooked and you have the desired texture, add the soy sauce and the other tablespoon of sesame oil.

Meanwhile, poach the eggs. Bring a saucepan of water to a rolling boil and add a spoonful of vinegar. Crack the eggs into a saucer or small cup and gently tip into the water. Poach for 6 minutes and then remove with a slotted spoon and drain on paper towels.

Divide the rice between two bowls and top each one with flakes of the mackerel and a poached egg. Garnish with the shallot and radish slices and sprigs of lemon verbena.

SNACKS & CONDIMENTS

BLISS BALLS

You can store these balls in the refrigerator for up to 5 days. They are great as a snack for when you feel like having a treat or need a burst of energy, and are particularly good for days when you are exercising.

¾ cup whole almonds

3 tablespoons flaxseeds

⅓ cup desiccated coconut, plus extra for rolling

¼lb dried apple, soaked in hot water for 1 minute and then drained

1 teaspoon ground turmeric

½ teaspoon ground cinnamon

1 tablespoon raw cacao powder

2 tablespoons coconut oil, melted

2 tablespoons raw liquid honey (or use the Turmeric Honey on page 15 and omit the turmeric above)

Put all the ingredients into a food processor and blend to a paste.

Roll into balls about the size of a walnut and then coat with the extra desiccated coconut.

SPICED AND ROASTED SEEDS

The orange juice adds a sweetness to this savory snack. The seeds are great for taking in a container to the office, or you can use them to add crunch to soups and salads.

¾ cup pumpkin seeds

¾ cup sunflower seeds

1 tablespoon olive oil

juice of 1 lime

juice of 1 orange

½ teaspoon ground turmeric

½ teaspoon mild chili powder

½ teaspoon sea salt flakes

Preheat the oven to 350°F and line a baking pan with nonstick parchment paper.

Mix all the ingredients together in a bowl and then spread out over the lined pan. Roast for 30 to 40 minutes, shaking the seeds halfway through cooking, until golden and crunchy.

Let cool and transfer to an airtight jar, seal, and store until needed.

TURMERIC AND BLACK PEPPER OATCAKES

A little turmeric goes a long way, especially when you see the rich
color of these oatcakes.

2 cups porridge oats
1 tablespoon olive oil
¼ teaspoon ground turmeric
good pinch of ground black
  pepper
¼ teaspoon sea salt flakes
flour, for dusting

Preheat the oven to 350°F and line a large baking pan
with nonstick parchment paper.

Put the oats into a large bowl. Add the olive oil,
turmeric, pepper, and sea salt and stir to combine.

Fill a pitcher with half boiled, half cool water. Add
enough of it to the oats to make them sticky enough
to form a ball that binds together. If you add too much
water, just add some more oats. Roll out the ball on a
lightly floured surface to a large rectangle about
¼ inch in thickness. Use a round cookie cutter (about
2½ inches in diameter) to cut circles. Use a spatula to
lift them onto the prepared baking pan.

Bake until golden, for 20 to 30 minutes, depending on
thickness. Transfer to a wire rack to cool.

TURMERIC HUMMUS

For a quicker version of this recipe, you can simply stir a little ground turmeric and lemon zest into ready-made hummus though, it must be said, there's something about making your own that can't be beaten.

14oz can chickpeas, rinsed and
  drained
zest and juice of 1 lemon
1 teaspoon sweet paprika
1 teaspoon ground turmeric
½ teaspoon mild chili powder
⅓ cup extra virgin olive oil, plus
  extra for drizzling
2 tablespoons tahini
1 teaspoon sea salt flakes
2 tablespoons water (or more
  if needed)

To serve
honey, for drizzling (optional)
Spiced and Roasted Seeds
  (see page 30)
a handful of microherbs
Turmeric and Black Pepper
  Oatcakes (see page 31),
  (optional)

Put all the ingredients in a food processor and blend until smooth, scraping down the insides of the processor as you go. Add more water if needed to get the right consistency.

Transfer to a bowl and add a drizzle of honey or olive oil. Garnish with a sprinkling of spiced and roasted seeds and a handful of microherbs. Serve with turmeric and black pepper oatcakes, if liked.

TURMERIC BANANA BREAD

This is a really easy and tasty way to use up overripe bananas. This recipe uses spelt flour but you could just as easily use gluten-free flour. The coconut oil and bananas help keep it moist and it's delicious toasted with a little butter.

2 cups spelt flour

2 teaspoons baking powder

½ teaspoon baking soda

¾ teaspoon salt

1 teaspoon ground ginger

1 teaspoon ground turmeric

3 tablespoons coconut oil, melted

⅓ cup coconut sugar (or ⅓ cup soft light brown sugar)

1 teaspoon vanilla extract

3 to 4 ripe bananas, mashed

2 large eggs

butter, to serve

Preheat the oven to 350°F and oil or butter an 8 x 4-inch loaf pan.

Sift the flour, baking powder, baking soda, salt, ginger, and turmeric into a bowl. In another bowl, mix together the melted coconut oil, coconut sugar, vanilla extract, mashed bananas, and eggs. Combine the mixture with a fork until quite smooth with just a few banana lumps.

Add the wet ingredients to the dry and stir until just combined into an airy batter. Scrape the batter into the loaf pan and bake until a skewer inserted in the center comes out clean (about 50 to 60 minutes).

Let cool in the pan for 10 minutes and then run a knife around the edge of the loaf to release it; invert onto a wire rack to cool completely. Cut into slices and serve, toasted if liked, and spread with butter, or transfer to a cookie can and keep for 3 to 4 days.

◇◇◇◇◇◇

VEGETABLES PICKLED WITH TURMERIC

Pickled vegetables add a delightful sharpness and crunch and are great for enjoying with a slice of cheese or cold cuts on picnics.

7oz daikon radish, peeled

7oz carrots, peeled

7oz turnips

5 curry leaves per jar (fresh or dried)

1 red chile per jar, seeded and halved lengthwise

2 strips of lemon rind per jar

For the pickling liquor

1¼ quarts warm water

¾ cup rice wine vinegar

⅓ cup coconut or regular sugar

2 tablespoons salt

½ teaspoon ground turmeric

Start by sterilizing your pickling jars by pouring boiling hot water into them and letting them stand for several minutes. Pour the water out and let the jars air dry.

Quarter the daikon radish lengthwise so you have 4 long pieces, then cut each quarter into chunks. The carrots can be cut in half lengthwise and then cut into chunky half-moons. You can cut the turnips any way you like, as long as they are approximately the same size as the rest of the vegetables.

Divide them evenly between the jars but don't overpack them. Tuck the curry leaves, chiles, and strips of lemon rind into the jars alongside the vegetables.

For the pickling liquor heat the water and vinegar in a saucepan over very low heat until it is nearly hot. Add the sugar, salt, and turmeric and stir until dissolved.

Pour the liquor evenly among the jars to cover the vegetables. You may need to press the vegetables down slightly. Seal the jars and let stand in the refrigerator for 3 days to pickle. If you don't have 3 days to spare, you can bring the liquor to boil before pouring it onto the vegetables, sealing the jar, and letting it cool down. You may not get quite get the same flavor but you will still have decent pickled vegetables.

TURMERIC MUSTARD

When you have a few pickles and condiments on hand, you'll be able to
add the benefits of turmeric to your dishes without even thinking about it.

3½ tablespoons mustard seeds
  (white or mixed)
¾ cup mustard powder
2 teaspoons sea salt flakes
¾ cup water
3 tablespoons apple cider vinegar
1 teaspoon ground turmeric
2 tablespoons raw liquid honey

Mix together the mustard seeds, mustard powder, and
sea salt in a bowl and add the water, combining well. Set
aside for 10 minutes before stirring in the apple cider
vinegar, turmeric, and honey; mix well.

Transfer to an airtight jar, seal, and let stand overnight
in the refrigerator. This will keep for up to 6 months in
a sealed jar in the refrigerator.

TURMERIC-INFUSED OIL

When you have this oil on hand in the kitchen you can make quick dressings or simply
drizzle it over dishes both to add flavor and to give an immediate health boost.

1 cup avocado oil
1 cup extra virgin olive oil
2 tablespoons grated fresh
  turmeric (or use 2 heaped
  tablespoons ground turmeric)
1 teaspoon coarsely ground
  black pepper

Add all the ingredients to a glass bottle, seal, and shake.
Let infuse for 2 weeks before using.

SOUPS

GINGER AND TURMERIC CARROT SOUP

This is a quick and very tasty soup, perfect for a cold winter day.

---

1 tablespoon peanut oil
½ onion, chopped
1 teaspoon grated fresh
   ginger root
1 teaspoon grated fresh turmeric
   or ground turmeric
⅛ teaspoon ground black pepper,
   plus extra to season
½lb carrots, coarsely chopped
1¾ cups hot vegetable stock
⅓ cup cashews, coarsely chopped
½ teaspoon mild chili powder
sea salt flakes

Heat the oil in a saucepan over low–medium heat, add the onion, and sauté for about 10 minutes until soft. Add the ginger, turmeric, and black pepper and stir through before adding the carrots.

Continue to stir the carrots for another couple of minutes, then add the stock. Bring to a boil, then reduce the heat and let simmer for 10 to 15 minutes, or until the carrots can be easily pierced with a sharp knife.

Transfer the soup to a blender and process until smooth; taste and adjust the seasoning.

Mix the chopped cashew nuts with the mild chili powder and dry roast in a skillet for a few minutes over low heat.

Ladle the soup into bowls, scatter with the spiced cashews, and serve.

KITCHARI

This recipe is based on an Ayurvedic cleansing soup; if you are doing the cleanse, you eat only kitchari for a certain number of days. We've included it simply because it's a surprisingly delicious recipe.

½ cup green mung beans, rinsed
and soaked overnight
1 teaspoon ground turmeric
¼ teaspoon ground black pepper
1 sheet of kombu seaweed or
¼ teaspoon asafetida
1½ tablespoons butter
¼ teaspoon mustard seeds
¼ teaspoon cumin seeds
¼ teaspoon fennel seeds
¼ teaspoon nigella seeds
6 dried curry leaves
zest and juice of 1 lemon
sea salt

For the crispy onions (optional)
1 onion, sliced and separate
into rings
all-purpose flour, for dusting
vegetable oil, for frying

To serve
plain yogurt
chopped nuts
Spiced and Roasted Seeds
(*see* page 30)
pea shoots (use watercress if you
can't find pea shoots)

Rinse the mung beans a couple of times, drain, and put into a saucepan with 1 quart of water.

Add the turmeric, black pepper, and seaweed or asafetida and bring to a boil. Reduce to a low simmer and cook for about an hour, until the beans are soft.

Heat the butter in a skillet over medium heat and when bubbling, add the seeds, curry leaves, and lemon zest. When the seeds begin to pop, remove from the heat and carefully add to the kitchari. Add the lemon juice and sea salt to taste.

Take the kitchari off the heat, cover, and let rest for 5 to 10 minutes while you prepare the crispy onions (if using).

Heat the vegetable oil in a wok over high heat. Dip the onion rings in flour and then carefully lower into the hot oil with tongs. When they are golden and crispy remove from the pan and drain on paper towels.

Top the kitchari with any or all of the serving suggestions: crispy onions, a dollop of plain yogurt, some chopped nuts, spiced and roasted seeds, and pea shoots.

SQUASH AND COCONUT DHAL

Dhal is a great standby to have during the week, and the butternut squash added here makes it a really filling meal in a bowl. Tamari is not an everyday companion for dhal or turmeric, but it adds a lovely flavor.

1¼ cups yellow split peas, rinsed and drained

2½ cups vegetable stock

3½ cups diced butternut squash

2 tablespoons tamari

3 tablespoons coconut cream

2 tablespoons olive oil

2 teaspoons mustard seeds

1 onion, thinly sliced

1 teaspoon ground turmeric

Put the split peas into a saucepan with the stock, bring to a simmer, and cook gently for about 30 minutes. Add the squash, tamari, and coconut cream and cook for another 15 to 20 minutes until the squash is soft. If you prefer your soup smooth, transfer to a blender and process until smooth.

Heat the olive oil in a small skillet. Add the mustard seeds and stir until they start popping. Add the onion and cook for 10 minutes over low–medium heat until softened. Stir in the turmeric and let the mixture cook for a few more minutes.

Ladle the soup into bowls and top with the aromatic onions. Serve immediately.

BACON AND EGG-DROP MISO

This is a really quick soup, perfect for lunch or after exercising.
To make it vegetarian, leave out the bacon. It's just as good.

---

2 strips bacon, chopped into
　　small pieces
2 scallions, thinly sliced
2 teaspoons brown miso paste
½ teaspoon grated fresh turmeric
　　or ground turmeric
2 large handfuls of baby spinach
2 eggs, beaten

Heat a nonstick saucepan and fry the bacon over
medium heat, adding the scallions after a couple
of minutes.

Dissolve the miso paste in a little just-boiled water
and add to the pan, along with about 2 cups just boiled
water and the turmeric. Allow the flavors to infuse for
a couple of minutes before adding the spinach.

When the spinach has wilted down a little, slowly add
the beaten eggs to the soup, ideally through a slotted
spoon to help create ribbons.

As soon as the egg sets, remove from the heat, divide
between 2 bowls, and serve immediately.

CHICKEN KHAO SOI

This is a very hearty and warming soup. It looks like it has a lot of ingredients but once you have assembled them, making the curry paste is a case of just blitzing everything together in a blender. The result is an amazing combination of flavors. The paste will keep in the refrigerator for up to 14 days sealed in an airtight container so you can make it in advance and keep it on hand for when you feel like enjoying a bowl of noodles and vegetables.

2 teaspoons coconut oil

2 x 14oz cans coconut milk

2 cups chicken stock

4 chicken thighs or drumsticks

¼ cup Thai fish sauce

1 tablespoon sugar

vegetable oil, for frying

7oz firm tofu, cubed

cornstarch, for dusting

10½oz soba noodles

For the curry paste

4 dried red chiles

3 shallots, quartered

8 garlic cloves

1-inch piece of galangal, peeled
    and coarsely chopped (or
    1 teaspoon galangal paste)

1-inch piece of fresh ginger root,
    peeled and coarsely chopped

¾oz fresh cilantro, coarsely
    chopped

First make the curry paste. Rehydrate the dried chiles in about 3 tablespoons hot water for about 20 minutes until they are soft. Drain, reserving the liquid. Put the chiles into a blender with all the remaining paste ingredients (or a bowl if using a hand-held stick blender). Add some of the chili water and blend to a smooth paste.

Heat the coconut oil in a large, heavy saucepan and add the curry paste. Fry the paste over medium heat, stirring constantly, for about 3 to 4 minutes or until it has browned slightly.

Shake the cans of coconut milk well so the milk isn't split and add to the pan. Stir in well and then add the chicken stock. Bring to a boil, then reduce the heat and let simmer for a further 5 minutes.

Add the chicken thighs or drumsticks to the simmering liquid and cook the chicken for 25 to 30 minutes until tender. Remove the meat and let cool for a few minutes. Shred the meat off the bone so you have some chunks and some finely shredded meat (rustic is the aim).

1 tablespoon ground coriander

1 tablespoon ground turmeric

1 teaspoon curry powder

To garnish

wilted tatsoi

a couple of handfuls of toasted
cashews

fresh sprigs of cilantro

sliced scallions

juice of 1 lime

Return the meat to the sauce, along with the Thai fish
sauce and the sugar.

Meanwhile, heat some vegetable oil in a skillet or wok
over medium–high heat. Dust the tofu cubes lightly
with cornstarch and then fry for a few minutes until
golden brown on all sides. Remove from the pan and
drain on paper towels.

Cook the soba noodles according to the package
directions, then drain. Portion the noodles, chicken,
and fried tofu into 4 soup bowls, then add the soup
to cover. Finish each bowl with some wilted tatsoi, a
handful of toasted cashews, some sprigs of cilantro,
scallion slices, and a squeeze of lime juice.

RASAM
WITH SASHIMI AND WILTING GREENS

There is a bit of theater in this dish as you pour the rasam broth over the fish and greens at the table. Alternatively, you could poach the salmon in the broth for a few minutes. Passing the rasam through a sieve gives you a clear broth that is filled with flavor.

3 tablespoons tamarind paste

3¼ cups hot water (from a just-boiled kettle)

1 tomato, quartered

14oz piece of good-quality skinless salmon, very thinly sliced on an angle

¼ cup Greek yogurt

¼lb baby spinach

¼lb baby kale

For the rasam paste

½ teaspoon cracked black pepper

1 teaspoon ground turmeric

4 dried red chiles

1 teaspoon cumin seeds

4 garlic cloves

¾oz cilantro stems

For the temper

1 teaspoon coconut oil

1 teaspoon black mustard seeds

½ teaspoon cumin seeds

10 to 12 dried curry leaves

¼ teaspoon asafetida

First put the tamarind paste and hot water into a large saucepan and let steep for about 10 minutes.

Meanwhile, start making the rasam paste by pounding all the ingredients together in a mortar and pestle until they form a coarse paste. Alternatively, you can blitz the ingredients coarsely in a blender, but the idea is to keep the paste coarse.

By this time, the tamarind should be soft. Mix the tamarind water with the paste, add the tomato, and place over low–medium heat to start to warm through.

For the temper, heat the coconut oil in a skillet over medium heat. Add the mustard seeds and, once they start popping, add the cumin. Let the cumin brown slightly (30 seconds or so). Add the curry leaves and asafetida and stir for several seconds. Add to the broth in the pan, bring to a boil, then reduce the heat and let the mixture simmer for 5 to 6 minutes. Remove from the heat and strain the rasam, pressing on the tomatoes to get all the flavor.

Add a tablespoon of yogurt to each bowl, along with some spinach and baby kale, and top with 3 or 4 slices of salmon. Bring the rasam back to a boil, serve the bowls at the table, and pour the piping hot rasam over the fish.

COCONUT CHICKEN SOUP
WITH TURMERIC AND KALE

The sweetness of coconut goes very well with turmeric. Here, the use of coconut water as opposed to coconut milk creates a light, fresh, and healthy soup that warms both body and soul.

1 tablespoon coconut oil, divided

1 small onion, chopped

1 cup coconut water

1 cup hot chicken stock

1 teaspoon grated fresh turmeric
 or ground turmeric

¼ teaspoon ground black pepper

¼lb kale, stalks removed and
 leaves shredded

1 Little Gem lettuce, halved

1 tablespoon olive oil

3½oz leftover roast chicken

squeeze of lemon juice, to taste
 (optional)

sea salt flakes

Melt half the coconut oil in a heavy saucepan, add the onion, and sauté over medium heat until soft, about 8 to 10 minutes. Add the coconut water, stock, turmeric, and black pepper. Keep the mixture at a low simmer.

Heat the remaining coconut oil in a skillet or wok and sauté the kale with a good pinch of sea salt for a few minutes until softened.

Place a griddle pan over high heat, brush the Little Gem halves with the olive oil, and griddle on both sides for 2 to 3 minutes.

Place the kale, lettuce, and chicken into bowls and pour in the hot coconut chicken stock to cover. Add lemon juice to taste, if liked. Serve immediately.

VEGETARIAN DISHES

CORN ON THE COB
WITH TURMERIC BUTTER

This is perfect for a summer barbecue. Adding the spices to the butter gives
an extra element of flavor. If you are using fresh cobs of corn, you will need
to boil them for about 10 minutes before grilling.

---

4 frozen or fresh cobs of corn
¾ stick unsalted butter
½ teaspoon grated fresh turmeric
　　or ground turmeric
½ teaspoon ground cumin
sea salt and ground black pepper

Either on a barbecue or a griddle pan, cook the corn
until soft and a little charred.

Melt the butter in a small saucepan and add the turmeric
and cumin. Cook the spices for a few minutes in the
butter to allow the flavors to infuse.

Serve the corn drizzled with the melted butter and
seasoned generously with salt and pepper.

NEW POTATO SALAD
WITH TURMERIC TAHINI DRESSING

Potato salad is given a novel twist here, replacing the usual mayo with
a vibrant tahini and turmeric dressing.

1lb 2oz new potatoes, washed

leaves from ½ bunch of fresh mint

4 scallions, thinly sliced on
    the diagonal

1 teaspoon sumac

sea salt and ground black pepper

For the dressing

⅓ cup tahini

juice of 1 lemon

2 tablespoons extra virgin olive oil

2 tablespoons water

1 teaspoon ground turmeric

Put the potatoes in a large pan and fill with enough
cold water to cover them fully. Add a small handful
of salt and 2 sprigs of the mint to the water before
covering with a lid. Place over high heat and bring to
a boil. Reduce the heat slightly and let simmer until
the potatoes are easily pierced with a sharp knife.

Remove from the heat and let cool slightly—it's best
to serve the salad warm but not piping hot.

In the meantime, make the dressing for the potatoes.
Pour the tahini, lemon juice, olive oil, water, and
turmeric into a large bowl and beat until smooth. If it
looks like the oil is separating, just add a teaspoon of
water at a time until the dressing is thick and glossy.
Season with a generous pinch of salt and pepper.

Toss the warm potatoes in the dressing, then add the
chopped mint leaves and sliced scallions. Toss gently
again until thoroughly combined. Tip into a serving
bowl and sprinkle with sumac to serve.

ROAST EGGPLANT
WITH TOFU AND TURMERIC DENGAKO

This is vegan heaven. Combining the tofu and coconut milk creates a creamy dressing while the miso turmeric dengako glaze gives an umami flavor to the eggplant. It's a salad to impress friends with.

2 to 3 eggplants (depending on size), sliced into 1-inch disks

olive oil, for dressing

1 tablespoon white miso

2 tablespoons cooking sake

1 teaspoon ground turmeric

1 tablespoon light brown sugar

¼lb kale, tough stems removed and leaves coarsely chopped

1 tablespoon soy sauce

1 teaspoon soft light brown sugar

7oz firm tofu

3 tablespoons coconut milk

sea salt and ground black pepper

To garnish

purple basil (optional)

2 tablespoons mixed chopped nuts

pea shoots (use watercress if you can't find pea shoots)

Preheat the oven to 450°F.

Put the eggplants in a large bowl and toss with plenty of olive oil and some sea salt. Arrange the disks on a large roasting pan.

Whisk the miso, sake, turmeric, and sugar together to make a loose paste. Brush the eggplant disks with the paste and roast in the oven for about 20 minutes until softened and deep golden in color, turning and brushing again with the paste halfway through. Remove from the oven and let cool a little.

Meanwhile, toss the kale with a little soy sauce and brown sugar and spread it out on a baking pan. As soon as you have removed the eggplant from the oven, add the kale and turn the oven off to allow the kale to get crisp in the residual heat while you arrange the salad.

Blitz the tofu with the coconut milk, either in a food processor or with a hand-held stick blender, for just a few seconds to create a creamy, crumbly texture.

Arrange the eggplant disks on a salad platter and scatter with the tofu and then the crispy kale. Finish with some purple basil, if using, chopped nuts, a few pea shoots (or some watercress), and a grinding of black pepper.

SWEET POTATO BULGUR

Grain salads are a great choice for a lunchbag or sharing platter because the grain makes it feel more filling. You can mix and match your grains and roasted vegetables, for example, carrots with freekeh or butternut squash wedges with cracked wheat.

1 large sweet potato, coarsely chopped

1½ teaspoons ground turmeric

1 teaspoon cumin seeds

2 to 3 tablespoons olive oil

½ cup bulgur wheat

1 teaspoon bouillon powder

¼lb baby spinach (shredded) or baby kale

2 tablespoons extra virgin olive oil

zest and juice of ½ lime

3 tablespoons baked kefir or plain yogurt

sea salt

fresh cilantro leaves, to serve

Preheat the oven to 425°F.

Put the potatoes in a large bowl with 1 teaspoon of the ground turmeric, the cumin seeds, olive oil, and a good pinch of salt and mix together. Transfer to a roasting pan and roast for about 20 minutes until the sweet potatoes are soft and a little crisp at the edges. Turn halfway through cooking.

Place the bulgur wheat in a saucepan, cover with 1 quart of water, and add the bouillon and remaining ground turmeric. Bring to a boil, then reduce the heat and let simmer for 10 to 12 minutes until cooked. Drain.

Toss the bulgur and roast sweet potato together with the spinach or kale and some extra virgin olive oil in a large bowl. Transfer to a salad platter.

Mix the lime zest and juice into the kefir or yogurt. Drizzle the salad with the mixture, then scatter with the picked cilantro leaves. Serve warm or let cool and then chill in the refrigerator until needed.

FIVE VEGETABLE TAGINE

This recipe does have quite a long list of ingredients, but the process is fairly simple and results in a great depth of flavor. Many of the spices are things that you can keep in your kitchen cupboard, but feel free to mix and match along with the vegetables. This recipe works really well in big batches that you can keep in the refrigerator and then simply heat up later in the week.

½ tablespoon ground turmeric

½ tablespoon ground ginger

½ tablespoon dried red chile flakes

½ tablespoon ground cumin

½ tablespoon ground coriander

seeds of 4 cardamom pods

1 garlic clove, crushed

juice of 1 lemon

½ cup olive oil

2 carrots, cut into wedges

½ butternut squash, peeled and
   cut into bite-sized pieces

2 small turnips, cut into wedges

½ celery root, peeled and cut into
   bite-sized pieces

1 eggplant, cut into ¾-inch dice

14oz can chickpeas, rinsed and
   drained

2 cups vegetable stock

1 tablespoon tomato paste

sea salt and ground black pepper

couscous and plain yogurt,
   to serve

Preheat the oven to 400°F.

Mix together all the spices, garlic, lemon juice, and olive oil in a bowl and season with salt and pepper. Add all the vegetables and mix thoroughly.

Place a large Dutch oven over medium heat and add the vegetables so that they temper for a few minutes. Now add the chickpeas, vegetable stock, and tomato paste. Give everything a stir, cover, and put in the oven for 30 to 40 minutes until the vegetables are cooked and the flavors have all infused.

Prepare your couscous and spoon into bowls. Ladle the tagine over the couscous and serve drizzled with a spoonful of plain yogurt.

YELLOW RICE
WITH COCONUT HALLOUMI

This coconut-fried halloumi is a winner every time and is a very nice treat with a bowl of hot, steaming yellow rice.

---

zest of 1 lemon

1 teaspoon ground turmeric

1 teaspoon ground ginger

2 teaspoons yellow mustard seeds

¾ cup basmati rice, rinsed

½ pint hot vegetable stock

8 kaffir lime leaves

3½oz halloumi cheese, cubed

flour, for dusting

1 egg, beaten

1 cup coconut flakes

vegetable oil, for frying

apple blossom flowers, to garnish
  (or use mint sprigs)

Dry-fry the lemon zest, turmeric, ginger, and yellow mustard seeds in a saucepan until the seeds begin to pop. Add the rice, stock, and kaffir lime leaves and bring to a boil, then reduce the heat and simmer for 10 minutes, or until the rice is fluffy and cooked and all the liquid has been absorbed.

For the halloumi, dip the cubes first into some flour, then the beaten egg, and finally coconut flakes, pressing to coat on all sides.

Heat the vegetable oil for shallow-frying in a wok and fry the coconut halloumi cubes until golden brown on all sides. Carefully remove with a slotted spoon and place on paper towels to drain away the excess oil.

Fluff up the rice with a fork and top with the fried halloumi. Garnish with apple blossom, if using, and serve immediately.

ROAST CAULIFLOWER SALAD
WITH GINGER, TURMERIC, AND LIME DRESSING

Roasting cauliflower whole is now a popular technique because it's a simple way to cook this versatile vegetable that gives it a lovely sweetness. The turmeric is in the dressing, which you toss the cauliflower in before serving with quinoa, and scallion and fresh cilantro to finish.

---

1 medium cauliflower

¼ cup olive oil, divided

1 teaspoon yellow mustard seeds

1 teaspoon fennel seeds

1 teaspoon ground coriander

1 teaspoon ground cumin

1 teaspoon ground turmeric

juice of 1 lime

2-inch piece of fresh ginger root, peeled and grated

½ cup mixed quinoa

3 scallions, thinly sliced diagonally

sea salt flakes

To garnish

handful of cilantro leaves

handful of Thai basil leaves (optional)

Spiced and Roasted Seeds (see page 30; optional)

Preheat the oven to 425°F.

To roast the cauliflower whole, simply place in a roasting pan, drizzle with half the olive oil, and sprinkle with sea salt. Roast for 45 to 60 minutes, or until the cauliflower is golden in color and can be easily pierced with a sharp knife. Remove from the oven and let cool a little before slicing into thick "steaks."

Heat the remaining oil in a saucepan and add the mustard seeds, stirring for about 1 minute over medium-high heat until the seeds begin to pop. Add the fennel seeds, coriander, cumin, and turmeric. Cook, stirring, for another minute or so until fragrant. Remove the pan from the heat and mix in the lime juice and ginger. Let cool and season with salt.

Mix the cauliflower in the dressing in a large bowl (don't worry if the cauliflower breaks up into florets) and let marinate while you cook the quinoa according to the package directions. Drain and set aside to cool.

Mix the quinoa into the cauliflower and dressing and arrange on a salad platter. Scatter with the sliced scallion, fresh cilantro, Thai basil, and spiced and roasted seeds, if using, just before serving.

BUDDHA BOWL

The idea of the Buddha bowl is to have something plant-based from each of the main food groups—in other words some protein, good carbohydrates, healthy fats, and plenty of fresh vegetables. With this recipe you get all that goodness plus the added benefits of some turmeric thrown in. The trick here is to cook the individual elements of the bowl separately so that you can enjoy all the layers and flavors.

½ cup cooked Yellow Rice (*see* page 64) or cooked basmati rice

unsalted butter or coconut oil, for frying

1 roasted garlic clove (wrap a whole garlic bulb with some sea salt in foil and roast in a low oven for 1 hour)

2oz mixed oriental mushrooms

1 tablespoon white wine

½ teaspoon harissa

2oz baby spinach

2oz green beans

1 teaspoon grated fresh turmeric or ground turmeric

1oz firm tofu

1 black radish, scrubbed and thinly sliced

½ teaspoon grated fresh ginger root or ground ginger

¼ Chinese cabbage, shredded

sea salt flakes

Cook the rice and keep warm in a low oven at approximately 300°F.

Melt about 1 teaspoon butter or coconut oil in a hot skillet and squeeze the roasted garlic clove into the pan. Stir for a few moments before adding the mushrooms, tossing continuously until golden and cooked. Deglaze the skillet with the white wine, transfer to a bowl, and set beside the rice in the oven to keep warm.

In the same skillet, fry off the harissa and add the baby spinach to wilt, then toss in the harissa. Set aside.

Heat a little coconut oil in a skillet and add the green beans, turmeric, and tofu, along with a little salt, scrambling the tofu as you cook the beans. Remove from the pan and set aside.

Lastly, for the vegetables, melt a little more butter or coconut oil with the grated ginger and wilt the Chinese cabbage for a minute or two.

Assemble your bowl with all the elements and serve.

BHINDI MASALA CURRY

This is a lightly spiced North Indian dish using the rather unheralded okra, which you do have to be careful not to overcook because they turn slimy. They're delicious in this traditional vegetable curry.

2 tablespoons coconut oil

10½oz okra, each sliced on an
    angle into 2–3 pieces

1 large onion, finely diced

1 bay leaf

1 teaspoon ground turmeric

½ teaspoon chili powder

½ teaspoon ground coriander

½ teaspoon ground cumin

1 cup water

¼ cup chopped fresh cilantro

sea salt

rice or Indian bread, to serve

For the tomato paste

3 ripe tomatoes

½-inch piece of fresh ginger root,
    peeled and coarsely chopped

4 garlic cloves

2 green chiles

2 cloves

½ teaspoon ground cinnamon

2 tablespoons plain yogurt

For the tomato paste, put the tomatoes, ginger, garlic, and chiles in a food processor and blend together until completely smooth. Crush the cloves with the cinnamon and add to the paste. Stir in the yogurt and set aside.

Melt half the coconut oil in large skillet over low heat and fry the okra for 10 to 15 minutes until almost cooked. It should still be firm but slightly browned all over. Remove from the pan and drain on paper towels.

In the same skillet, add the remaining coconut oil and fry the onion with the bay leaf until completely soft and slightly caramelized. Add the ground spices and stir quickly so as not to burn them. Stir in the tomato paste and keep cooking over low heat until the sauce has thickened. Add the water, season with salt, and give it a very good stir. Return the okra to the sauce and cook for another 5 minutes. Do not cook for longer otherwise the okra will become extremely slimy.

Add the chopped cilantro and serve with rice or a good Indian bread to soak up the sauce.

TURMERIC GNOCCHI

Seaweed and turmeric make a surprisingly good combination. You don't need to go to all the trouble of making your own gnocchi for this recipe but you will notice the difference if you have the time and patience to give it a try.

4 large russet potatoes

1¼ cups all-purpose flour, plus extra for dusting

2 teaspoons sea salt flakes

1 egg, beaten

1 stick unsalted butter, at room temperature and cut into small cubes

½ teaspoon ground turmeric

1 teaspoon nori or dulse seaweed flakes

1 tablespoon vegetable oil

2oz pecorino cheese (or any hard cheese), grated

handful of fresh chives, snipped

2 tablespoons Spiced and Roasted Seeds (see page 30) or toasted pumpkin seeds

pea shoots, to garnish (use watercress if you cannot get pea shoots)

ground black pepper

Preheat the oven to 425°F.

Bake the potatoes for about 45 minutes, or until easily pierced with a sharp knife. When just cool enough to handle, peel the potatoes and pass through a potato ricer into a bowl. (Or, mash until smooth and then push the mixture through a sieve.) Set aside to cool.

Sift the flour into the potatoes and sprinkle with the salt. Create a small well in the middle and add the beaten egg. Stir and mix together before tipping out onto a floured surface. Knead the mixture until it is soft and smooth, then divide in half, then again, and once more, so that you have 8 equal pieces. Now roll these into long sausage ropes and cut into pieces measuring about ¾ inch square.

Bring a saucepan of salted water to a boil and cook the gnocchi in batches. The gnocchi are ready when they float to the surface (usually after a few minutes). Remove with a slotted spoon and drain on paper towels.

When the gnocchi are cooked, melt the butter in a large skillet and add the turmeric and seaweed flakes. In a separate pan, add the vegetable oil and fry the gnocchi again in batches, and divide among 4 bowls. Drizzle with the flavored butter and scatter with grated cheese, chives, and toasted seeds. Finish with a few pea shoots and a grinding of black pepper and serve.

FISH & MEAT DISHES

TURMERIC SHRIMP LINGUINE

This is a wonderful sharing dish. The traditional Mediterranean flavors work really well with the addition of the turmeric and fresh yogurt sauce.

---

2 tablespoons olive oil, plus extra for drizzling

½ shallot, finely diced

1 garlic clove, grated or minced

1-inch piece of fresh ginger root, peeled and grated

1 teaspoon ground turmeric

7oz raw shrimp (ideally shell-on)

7oz linguine

¾ cup plain yogurt

2oz arugula

8 cherry tomatoes, halved

sea salt and ground black pepper

Fill a large saucepan with water, add a handful of salt, and place over high heat.

While the pasta water is coming to a boil, heat the oil in a skillet over low–medium heat. Add the shallot and fry slowly until it becomes transparent. Add the garlic and ginger and continue to fry over low heat until they are aromatic and soft, about 4 to 5 minutes. Add the turmeric and cook for another couple of minutes.

Increase the heat and add the shrimp, stirring to coat them in the other ingredients, and cook for 4 to 8 minutes.

By this time, the water should be boiling, so add the linguine and cook according to the package directions. Drain the pasta, reserving a cupful of the water, and stir a little oil through it.

Once the shrimp feel firm to touch and are pink all over, add the yogurt and half a ladleful of reserved pasta water. Cook, stirring, for 3 to 4 minutes to fully soak up the flavors, adding more water if necessary.

Season to taste and reduce the heat to very low. Add the pasta, arugula, and tomatoes and stir through until the arugula has wilted. The pasta will soak up the sauce. If it looks a little dry add some more pasta water until you have a sauce that coats every strand. Serve immediately.

SALMON GLAZED
WITH MISO & TURMERIC
WITH WILTED GREENS

The glaze for the salmon lifts this simple and healthy weeknight dinner
to create something special. Salmon is full of healthy Omega oils,
which have a very important role in maintaining cells.

2 tablespoons mirin

1 teaspoon coconut sugar (or use
brown sugar)

1 garlic clove, roasted (*see* page 68)

1 teaspoon brown miso paste

1 teaspoon Turmeric Honey (*see*
page 15, or use liquid honey)

1 tablespoon light sesame oil

2 x 5½oz pieces skin-on salmon

1 tablespoon unsalted butter

½ teaspoon ground turmeric

⅛ teaspoon ground black pepper

1 bok choy, leaves separated

3½oz snow peas

3½oz cavolo nero, stalks removed
and leaves chopped

few slices of sushi ginger

2 tablespoons soy sauce

To make the glaze, whisk together the mirin, sugar,
garlic, miso paste, and honey.

Preheat the broiler to high. Place a nonstick skillet
(with a heatproof handle) over medium–high heat, add
the sesame oil and fry the salmon skin-side down until
the skin is golden and crisp. Turn over, brush with the
miso turmeric glaze, and place the skillet under the
broiler for a few minutes.

Heat another large skillet or a wok over high heat and
add the butter, turmeric, and black pepper. Add the
bok choy, snow peas, and cavolo nero. Toss for about
30 seconds, then add the sushi ginger and soy sauce.

When the greens are wilted, divide between 2 plates
and top with the glazed salmon.

KERALAN FISH CURRY

With the combination of spices, this is a gentle but warming curry from the Ayurvedic tradition, balanced by the coconut milk and lemon. It's a lovely fresh dish and you can use any firm, white-fleshed fish that is in season.

1 tablespoon peanut oil

1-inch piece of cinnamon stick

3 cloves

⅓ teaspoon mustard seeds

⅓ teaspoon fennel seeds

5 black peppercorns

½ onion, thinly sliced

7 dried curry leaves

¾ cup basmati rice

1½ teaspoons garlic paste

1½ teaspoons ginger paste

¼ teaspoon ground turmeric

pinch of sea salt

½ cup water

½ cup coconut milk

squeeze of lemon juice

9oz firm monkfish (or cod),
    cut into large cubes

1 teaspoon unsalted butter or
    coconut oil

2¾oz monk's beard or samphire
    (or use baby spinach)

Heat the oil in a large nonstick saucepan, add the whole spices, and cook over medium heat until the mustard seeds start popping. Add the onion and curry leaves and cook for a few minutes until soft and translucent.

Meanwhile, cook the rice following the package directions.

Add the garlic and ginger pastes to the spices and stir for a minute. Add the turmeric, salt, and water. Bring to a boil, then reduce the heat and simmer for about 7 minutes until nicely reduced. Add the coconut milk, bring back to a boil, and cook for a couple of minutes.

Squeeze in the lemon juice and add the fish in one layer, just covering with the sauce. Simmer gently until the fish is cooked through, about 8 minutes (depending on the thickness of the fish). Taste for seasoning.

Heat the butter or coconut oil in a small skillet and sauté the monks beard or samphire for a minute or two.

Serve the curry on the rice, scattered with the greens.

SERVES 2

◇◇◇◇◇◇

COD WITH TURMERIC AND TAMARIND

This recipe marries turmeric with the cod and the honey in the salad dressing.
The salad is raw, giving freshness and crunch to complement the gently cooked fish.

1 tablespoon tamarind paste

½ teaspoon grated fresh turmeric
or ground turmeric

1 tablespoon hot water

2 x 7oz pieces skin-on cod
(ask your fishdealer to
remove any bones)

½ onion, grated

good splash of rose or jasmine tea

lime wedges, to serve

For the salad

½ white cabbage, finely chopped
or grated

½ small cucumber (ideally
Lebanese), sliced

½ red onion, thinly sliced

handful of any soft fresh herbs,
such as basil, mint, or dill

1 teaspoon black onion seeds

2 teaspoons manuka honey
(or use raw honey)

3 tablespoons plain yogurt

sea salt and ground black pepper

Stir the tamarind paste, turmeric, and hot water together in a large bowl to combine and then set aside to cool. Add the fish to the marinade, toss gently to coat, and then add the grated onion. Let chill in the refrigerator for 20 minutes.

Toss together all of the salad ingredients in a bowl until combined. Season with salt and pepper and set aside.

Get a nonstick skillet really hot and then place the cod skin-side down in the pan. Cook for 3 minutes, then turn the fish over and add a splash of tea. After the initial whoosh of the tea hitting the skillet, reduce the heat, cover, and let steam for about 5 minutes.

Pile the salad onto plates and serve the fish on top, served with lime wedges for squeezing.

MUSSELS
WITH TURMERIC AND LEMONGRASS

Mussels are wonderful for sharing, so simple to cook, and can take on lots of strong flavors. In this case the combination of turmeric, chile, and lemongrass works beautifully.

2 tablespoons coconut oil

4 garlic cloves, sliced

2 red chiles, seeded and
   thinly sliced

1 stick of lemongrass, crushed
   along the stem and halved

½ teaspoon ground turmeric

2¼lb fresh mussels, cleaned and
   beards removed

14oz cherry tomatoes, halved

1 bunch of fresh Thai basil (or use
   red basil or regular basil)

sea salt and ground black pepper

Heat the coconut oil in a large, wide saucepan with a lid over low–medium heat and add the garlic, chiles, and lemongrass. Fry for a few minutes until they are aromatic and the garlic begins to brown slightly. Add the turmeric and cook for another 30 seconds.

Increase the heat to high and add the mussels and tomatoes. Season with salt and pepper, stir everything together, and cover the pan. Shake every now and again so the mussels are nudged open (this should take approximately 4 to 5 minutes).

Give the last few mussels a chance to open if they haven't already. If any remain firmly shut, make sure you discard them before serving. When they're all opened you should have a lovely broth at the bottom made from the mussel and tomato juices.

Serve on a large sharing platter scattered with plenty of Thai basil.

BEEF STEW

Adding turmeric to stews is a simple way to introduce a little more of this healthy spice into your cooking. Along with the ginger, it adds a touch of warmth to this hearty beef stew. Feel free to use any seasonal root vegetables or tubers you have on hand, such as parsnips, squash, turnips, or celery root.

olive oil, for frying

2 onions, sliced

14oz beef for stew, cut into chunks and seasoned with salt and pepper

1 teaspoon ground turmeric

1 teaspoon ground ginger

6 shallots, halved

12 baby carrots

8 baby turnips

1 quart vegetable stock (or enough to cover the meat)

Parmesan cheese rind (if you have one)

hunks of sourdough bread, to serve

Preheat the oven to 300°F.

Heat a little olive oil in a large Dutch oven over low-medium heat and add the onions. Gently fry until softened. Remove from the pot, add a little more oil, and start browning the steak in batches.

Return the meat and the onions to the Dutch oven and add the turmeric and ginger. Cook slowly over low heat for 10 minutes.

Add the shallots, carrots, turnips, vegetable stock, and Parmesan rind, if using. Cover and place in the oven for 3 hours. Check on it occasionally to make sure there is enough liquid to cover the meat and vegetables. If at any time it looks as if it is getting dry, top it off with stock or a little water.

Serve with hunks of crusty sourdough bread to mop up the flavorsome juices.

MASSAMAN BEEF LARB

Larb is a Southeast Asian dish that is particularly popular in Laos and is made with ground beef and served in lettuce leaves. In this recipe it is deconstructed and paired with the fragrant massaman Thai curry paste. You can buy massaman paste in the supermarket but, for a really fresh taste, why not make your own? You can also use any type of ground meat you like as an alternative to beef. Pork, chicken, or duck would all work well.

14oz ground beef, seasoned with
  salt and pepper
1 tablespoon massaman paste
  (see below)
1 tablespoon peanut oil
2 shallots, chopped
½ cup hot vegetable stock
1 cup couscous
1 tablespoon extra virgin olive oil

For the massaman paste
(makes 1 small jar)
8 garlic cloves
2 sticks of lemongrass, outer layers
  removed, thinly sliced
1 shallot, sliced
1-inch piece of fresh ginger root,
  peeled and sliced
1 tablespoon sesame oil
seeds of 4 cardamom pods
1 tablespoon coriander seeds
1 teaspoon cumin seeds

First make the paste. Preheat the oven to 350°F and toss the garlic, lemongrass, shallot, and ginger with the sesame oil. Spread out over a baking pan and roast for 8 minutes, tossing the ingredients halfway through the cooking time. Let cool.

Meanwhile, combine the cardamom pods and coriander and cumin seeds in a small nonstick skillet and toast over medium heat until fragrant, about 2 minutes. Let the spices cool before crushing them in a spice mill or using a mortar and pestle.

Tip the roasted garlic, lemongrass, shallot, and ginger into a food processor and add the ground spices and all the remaining paste ingredients. Blitz to a paste, adding a little olive oil if the mixture is too dry. The paste can be made in advance and kept in the refrigerator for up to a month.

Tip the ground beef into a large bowl, add the tablespoon of massaman paste, and mix together. Let marinate for 30 minutes, if you have time.

1 teaspoon ground turmeric

½ teaspoon ground cinnamon

¼ teaspoon ground cloves

½ teaspoon sea salt flakes

small bunch of fresh cilantro stems

1 teaspoon chile paste (or to taste)

To serve

mixed salad leaves

fresh picked thyme

Turmeric-infused Oil (*see* page 37)

Heat the oil in a large skillet and sauté the shallots over medium heat until soft, about 5 minutes. Remove from the heat and set aside while you brown the ground beef in the same pan. Once the ground beef is browned, return the onions to the pan along with the hot vegetable stock and let simmer for 15 to 20 minutes.

Put the couscous in a large bowl and add enough just-boiled water to cover. Drizzle in a little extra virgin olive oil and cover with plastic wrap or a plate for 5 minutes until the couscous has absorbed the water and can be easily fluffed with a fork.

Serve the couscous and larb with lots of fresh salad leaves and fresh thyme. Drizzle with a little turmeric-infused oil to finish.

ROAST CHICKEN
WITH TANDOORI RUB

The spices in this rub result in a subtle flavor that is not too heavy or overpowering, so this is definitely one to try the next time you want to roast a whole chicken.

1 large whole chicken

1 lemon

14oz purple sprouting broccoli

olive oil, for drizzling

½ teaspoon dried red chile flakes

3½oz baby kale or baby leaf salad

sea salt flakes

For the brine (optional)

4½ quarts cold water

¾ cup fine salt

1⅓ cups soft light brown sugar,
    not packed

For the tandoori paste

2 tablespoons coconut oil

½ teaspoon ground ginger

1 teaspoon ground cumin

1 teaspoon garam masala

½ teaspoon chili powder

½ teaspoon ground coriander

1 teaspoon ground turmeric

½ teaspoon ground black pepper

3 garlic cloves, crushed

Vigorously stir all the brine ingredients together until dissolved. Put the chicken into a stockpot or container big enough to hold it comfortably and pour in enough brine to cover. Let the chicken stand submerged in the brine for at least 3 hours but ideally overnight. Remove the chicken from the brine, rinse, and pat dry with paper towels. (You can skip the brining step if you are roasting the chicken on the day.)

Preheat the oven to 400°F.

Pound or blend all the paste ingredients together so you have a slightly thick rub.

Slice the lemon into four and rub the chicken all over, inside and out. Rub the paste all over the chicken, making sure you don't neglect the legs, thighs, and wings.

Put the lemon quarters into the cavity, place the chicken in a roasting pan, and cover with foil. Roast in the oven for 2 hours, then remove the foil, increase the heat to 475°F, and cook for another 20 minutes, or until well browned. Remove from the oven and let rest.

Steam the broccoli until cooked but still with some bite. Toss with a little olive oil, the chile flakes, and some sea salt. Serve the chicken with the broccoli and kale salad.

LAMB CUTLETS
IN TURMERIC COCONUT MARINADE

The turmeric coconut marinade used in this recipe infuses the meat with delicious flavors that perfectly complement the richness of the lamb. This is a stunning dish for cooking on the barbecue at the height of summer and is great served with a crisp, fresh, mixed leaf salad scattered with spiced and roasted seeds (*see* page 30). You could even drizzle your salad with a dressing based on the turmeric-infused oil on page 37.

4 lamb cutlets (about 4oz each)

mixed leaf salad, to serve

Spiced and Roasted Seeds
(*see* page 30), to serve

For the marinade

3 tablespoons creamed coconut

juice of ½ lemon

2 tablespoons vegetable oil

¼ cup water

½ cup coarsely chopped fresh
cilantro

½ shallot, quartered

2 garlic cloves

½ teaspoon ground cumin

½ teaspoon ground coriander

1½ teaspoons ground turmeric

Melt the creamed coconut in a saucepan over low heat until it becomes liquid. Add to a bowl with the remaining marinade ingredients and beat them all together until you have a thick, rich, glossy marinade. If the oils are separating, adding a little water or lemon juice will bring it back together again. You should end up with a beautiful yellow paste flecked with cilantro.

Coat the lamb cutlets in the marinade and then transfer the cutlets and all the marinade to a nonmetallic container or resealable plastic food bag and place in the refrigerator overnight to absorb the flavors. Technically, the longer the better, so you can leave them for up to 3 days in the refrigerator if you're planning ahead.

When you are ready to cook, make sure you take the cutlets out of the refrigerator well before you start cooking to allow them to return to room temperature and so the marinade melts again.

For the best results, a barbecue will cook the perfect lamb cutlets but otherwise a ridged grill pan is will do the job. Heat the pan to smoking point and then reduce

the heat to medium. After a couple of minutes, add
the lamb cutlets. Do not touch them so they get lovely
char marks (if you move them too much they will never
brown in a nice uniform way). Once they have char
marks on the one side, flip them over and do the same
again, increasing the heat if the pan has cooled slightly.

They are ready when both sides have nice char marks
and the meat next to the bone is springy and slightly
firm. Remove from the heat, cover with foil, and let rest
for at least 5 minutes.

Serve the lamb simply with a mixed leaf salad and some
spiced and roasted seeds.

SWEETS

TURMERIC MAPLE ICE CREAM

You don't need an ice-cream machine to make this recipe. If you do have a machine, then you can use your favorite base recipe and add the maple syrup and turmeric for flavoring. It's surprising but the turmeric really works with the cream.

1½ tablespoons maple syrup

1 teaspoon ground turmeric

2½ cups heavy cream

14oz can condensed milk

4 caramelized cookies (such as Lotus Biscoff), crushed into fine crumbs

Gently heat the maple syrup and turmeric together in a small saucepan for a few minutes, just to infuse the flavors. Remove from the heat and set aside to cool.

Put the cream and condensed milk into a large bowl and, using a hand-held electric beater, beat the mixture for 5 minutes or so until the mixture forms soft peaks.

Beat the turmeric-infused maple syrup into the cream and condensed milk mixture, then spoon into a rigid freezerproof container.

Let freeze overnight until firm. Transfer to the refrigerator for 15 to 20 minutes before scooping. Serve scattered with the cookie crumbs.

POPCORN

This is such a simple but popular snack. If you prefer savory instead of sweet, then just replace the maple syrup with ½ teaspoon ground cumin.

2 tablespoons coconut oil

1 cup popcorn kernels

½ teaspoon ground turmeric

¼ teaspoon dried red chile flakes

1 teaspoon sea salt flakes
  (or to taste)

2 tablespoons maple syrup

Place a large, deep, lidded saucepan over high heat. When the pan is hot, add the coconut oil and after about 30 seconds add the popcorn kernels.

Cover the pan and give it a shake so that the kernels are all coated in oil and getting the heat. It's a bit tricky to know when all the kernels have finished popping if you don't have a pan with a glass lid, but when the popping noise stops for a few seconds, have a look.

Tip into a bowl and sprinkle with the turmeric, dried chile flakes, and sea salt. Drizzle with the maple syrup and give the bowl a good shake until the seasoning is evenly distributed. Serve immediately.

TURMERIC CHAI MUFFINS

These muffins aren't overly sweet and they have a lovely soft texture, making them perfect for a weekend treat.

½ stick unsalted butter, softened

¾ cup light brown sugar, not packed

1 egg

½ teaspoon vanilla extract

1½ cups all-purpose flour

½ teaspoon salt

¾ teaspoon baking powder

¼ teaspoon baking soda

1 teaspoon ground cinnamon

½ teaspoon ground turmeric

½ teaspoon ground ginger

½ teaspoon ground cardamom

¼ teaspoon ground black pepper

½ cup milk (or nut milk of choice)

For the glaze

2 tablespoons butter, melted

½ cup confectioners' sugar, sifted

2 teaspoons milk (or nut milk
   of choice)

¼ teaspoon ground cinnamon

pinch of ground ginger

pinch of ground turmeric

pinch of ground cardamom

¼ teaspoon vanilla extract

Preheat the oven to 350°F, and line a muffin pan with 8 paper baking cups.

Cream the butter and sugar in a large bowl with a wooden spoon until pale and fluffy. Gradually add the egg and vanilla extract and mix until fully incorporated.

In a separate bowl, mix together all the dry ingredients including the spices. Add half the dry ingredients to the egg and sugar mixture and stir to combine. Add half the milk and mix in before adding and stirring in the remaining dry ingredients. Finally incorporate the rest of the milk until you have a smooth mixture.

Spoon the batter into each muffin case almost to the top. Bake for 20 to 25 minutes, or until the tops of the muffins are well risen and spring back when touched (or check with a skewer). Transfer to a wire rack to cool.

Meanwhile, combine all the glaze ingredients until smooth. Once the muffins have cooled slightly, after 5 to 10 minutes, dip their tops into the glaze and wait until it hardens. They can then be double-dipped if desired for extra flavor. Alternatively, you can drizzle the glaze over the tops of the muffins using a spoon.

MANGO AND TURMERIC NOBAKE CHEESECAKE

This delicious tropical cheesecake looks amazing with its cheery mango puree topping, and is really easy to make, requiring no baking whatsoever. A slice of this makes the perfect dessert after a curry because the cream cheese has a cooling effect on the palate. The health-conscious among you may wish to use reduced-fat cream cheese instead of full-fat. Either way, this cake is a real knockout.

For the base

9oz ginger snap cookies

¼ teaspoon ground black pepper

1 stick salted butter, melted

For the filling

1 large mango

2½ teaspoons ground turmeric, divided

14oz regular cream cheese (or use reduced-fat)

½ cup superfine sugar

1 cup heavy cream

¼ cup water

1 tablespoon powdered gelatin

Line an 8-inch round springform cake pan with nonstick parchment paper.

Make the cake crust by blitzing the gingersnap cookies and black pepper in a food processor until the consistency of fine crumbs. Add the melted butter and stir to incorporate. Press this mixture firmly into the bottom of the cake pan with the back of a spoon and let chill in the refrigerator for at least 30 minutes.

Make a mango puree by peeling the mango and blitzing all of its flesh in a food processor until smooth. Add ½ teaspoon of the ground turmeric and mix well.

In a bowl, beat the cream cheese, sugar, and remaining turmeric by hand with a spatula or wooden spoon until the sugar has dissolved. In a separate bowl, beat the cream until soft peaks form and set it aside.

Bloom the gelatin by putting ¼ cup of cold water into a small pan (this can also be done in a microwave in a plastic bowl). Slowly sprinkle the gelatin onto the

surface of the water and wait 5 minutes until it has absorbed the water and formed a slushy paste. Warm this paste over very low heat, just hot enough to melt the gelatin, stirring with a fork continuously until the granules have fully dissolved. Once they have dissolved, remove the liquid from the heat and beat it into the mango puree.

Beat two-thirds of the mango puree into the cream-cheese mixture, then carefully fold in the whipped cream until fully incorporated. Pour this mixture onto the chilled crust and smooth down the top with a metal spatula or knife. Return to the refrigerator and let chill and set for 1 to 2 hours.

Once the cheesecake has almost set, finish it by pouring the remaining mango puree over the top and smoothing it down with a metal spatula. Let the cake chill for 2 hours, or until fully set, before releasing it from the pan and slicing it to serve.

TURMERIC-GLAZED BANANAS
WITH ICE CREAM

This is the simplest of desserts. The turmeric
complements the sweetness of the bananas and
maple to give just the right balance.

2 tablespoons unsalted butter

1 teaspoon grated fresh turmeric

1 large or 2 small bananas, peeled
and sliced in half lengthwise

2 tablespoons maple syrup

2 scoops of vanilla ice cream or
coconut yogurt

Place a large skillet over medium heat and add the
butter. When the butter is foaming, add the turmeric
followed by the bananas, cut sides down. Let colour in
the butter and turmeric. Gently turn the banana halves
over in the butter to coat. After a couple of minutes, add
the maple syrup to thicken the sauce.

Serve hot with a scoop of vanilla ice cream or coconut
yogurt on the side.

COCONUT RICE PUDDING
WITH TURMERIC, LEMONGRASS, AND GINGER SYRUP

This is a variation on traditional rice pudding. The simple addition of coconut, turmeric, lemongrass, and ginger make it spiced and sweet at the same time.

2 x 14oz cans coconut milk

1 cup water

¾ cup Arborio or basmati rice, washed and drained

½ cup palm sugar or ¾ cup soft light brown sugar, not packed

1 stick of lemongrass, ends trimmed and outer layers removed and discarded

For the syrup

1½ cups water

1 teaspoon ground turmeric

2 sticks of lemongrass, ends trimmed and outer layers removed and discarded

1-inch piece of preserved stem ginger, thickly sliced into 4

pared rind and juice of 1 lime

pinch of ground black pepper

½ cup palm sugar or ¾ cup soft light brown sugar, not packed

To garnish (optional)

apple blossom flowers

few sprigs of lemon verbena

Start by making the syrup. Put the water, turmeric, lemongrass, ginger, lime rind, and pepper in a small saucepan and bring to a boil. Reduce to a simmer and let the syrup bubble away for 5 to 10 minutes, or until reduced by half.

Once reduced, strain the syrup into a bowl, discarding the contents of the sieve. Return the syrup to the pan, add the sugar, and bring this to a boil. Let the mixture reduce for about 5 minutes until syrupy. Remove from the heat and let the syrup cool. Then stir in 1 to 2 teaspoons of juice from the pared lime to taste. Set the syrup aside.

Add the coconut milk and water to a medium saucepan and bring to a boil. Then add the rice, sugar, and lemongrass and stir well. As soon as the liquid returns to a boil, reduce the heat to medium and cook the rice slowly for about 20 minutes, stirring occasionally so as not to scald the mixture. Once the rice is cooked but still has a slight bite, remove the pan from the heat and fish out and discard the lemongrass stalk.

Serve the rice pudding warm or cold, drizzled with a spoonful of the spiced syrup and garnished with apple blossom flowers and lemon verbena sprigs, if liked.

DRINKS

◇◇◇◇◇◇

APPLE TURMERIC TONIC

There is something incredibly refreshing about adding the slightly bitter turmeric and sharp lemon juice to sweet apple juice. For an extra shot of goodness, add a few drops of holy basil tincture, an adaptogen that helps your body to cope better with stress.

3¼ cups pressed apple juice

3 teaspoons grated fresh turmeric

3 teaspoons grated fresh
   ginger root

juice of 2 lemons

Put all the ingredients into a large pitcher or bowl and let stand for a few hours or overnight, if possible, to allow the flavors to infuse.

Strain into a large glass bottle, seal, and let chill in the refrigerator, where it will keep for up to 3 days.

Give the bottle a good shake before serving.

MAKES 2 CUPS

◇◇◇◇◇◇

CARROT AND ORANGE TONIC

Another refreshing chilled tonic that instantly makes you feel good in the morning.

1¼ cups freshly squeezed
   orange juice

¾ cup fresh carrot juice

juice of 2 lemons

2 teaspoons grated fresh turmeric
   or ground turmeric

2 teaspoons grated fresh
   ginger root

Put all the ingredients into a large pitcher or bowl and let stand for a few hours or overnight, if possible, to allow the flavors to infuse.

Strain into a glass bottle, seal, and let chill in the refrigerator, where it will keep for up to 3 days.

HOT TONIC

For a warming, health-boosting drink, add a little turmeric, some fresh ginger root, lemon slices, and raw honey to hot water. Fresh turmeric root is ideal for this infusion, but you can also use ground turmeric if you're having difficulty obtaining the fresh kind.

---

3 thin slices of fresh turmeric or
   ½ teaspoon ground turmeric
3 slices of fresh ginger root
2 slices of lemon
1 teaspoon raw honey

If using fresh turmeric, simply put all the ingredients in a mug and add boiling water. Stir to dissolve the honey and let stand for 5 minutes to allow the flavors to infuse before drinking.

If using ground turmeric, add the turmeric and ginger to a small pan of water, bring to a boil, and let simmer for a few minutes. You might want to add a pinch of black pepper or cayenne pepper. Remove from the heat, pour into a mug, add the lemon and honey, stir, and enjoy.

TURMERIC TODDY

Thyme is good for relieving a sore throat and combines well with the ginger, turmeric, honey, and lime in this hot tonic to boost your immune system. It's delicious any time but especially if you think you are catching a cold. If you're feeling brave, add a couple of crushed garlic cloves at the same time as the honey.

10g fresh thyme sprigs

½-inch piece of fresh ginger root, peeled and grated

1 teaspoon grated fresh turmeric or ground turmeric

¼ teaspoon black peppercorns

500ml water

2 tablespoons raw honey

juice of 1 lime

Use a rolling pin to lightly bash the thyme, which will help to release the oil.

Add the thyme, ginger, turmeric, peppercorns, and measured water to a saucepan and bring to just below boiling point. Reduce the heat to low and let the mixture simmer for 10 minutes.

Remove from the heat and add the honey and lime juice, stirring until the honey is dissolved. Strain and serve.

MAKES 1 LARGE POT

◇◇◇◇◇◇

TURMERIC TEA

This is a wonderfully refreshing tea, perfect to start the day with or as a pick-me-up in the afternoon. The addition of cinnamon makes it lovely and warming, although you could replace this with a teaspoon of green tea leaves as an alternative. For even more of a chai taste, replace the lemongrass with a few cloves and bashed cardamom pods.

1 quart water
½ cinnamon stick
1 stick of lemongrass, bashed
few slices of fresh ginger root
few slices of fresh turmeric
   or 1 heaped teaspoon
   ground turmeric
¼ teaspoon black peppercorns

Bring the water to a boil in a large saucepan.

Slowly add the herbs and spices and simmer gently for 10 minutes.

Strain into a teapot and serve.

GOLDEN MYLK

This is a traditional drink enjoyed in Indonesia. You can try it with or without the cinnamon, depending on your preference. Equally, you might prefer it without any maple syrup or honey.

1¼ cups almond or coconut milk
½ teaspoon ground turmeric
½ teaspoon ground cinnamon
pinch of ground black pepper
1 teaspoon coconut oil
1 teaspoon maple syrup (or honey)

Put the almond or coconut milk into a pan and heat gently over low heat.

Meanwhile, put the remaining ingredients in a small bowl, add a little boiled water, and stir to make a paste. Whisk this into the warming milk and then continue to heat gently for 5 minutes. It's then ready to serve.

SERVES 1

◇◇◇◇◇◇

TURMERIC CHAMPAGNE

This is a twist on a classic cocktail, the turmeric giving it a lovely golden hue.
There is no shaking involved here. Simply build the cocktail in the glass.

1 sugar cube
1 teaspoon turmeric juice (extracted
   from fresh turmeric root)
2 dashes of angostura bitters
1 tablespoon brandy
squeeze of lemon juice
Champagne, to top off
cape gooseberry or strip of lemon
   zest, to garnish

Put the sugar cube in the bottom of a Champagne flute
and add the remaining ingredients one at a time.

Garnish the glass with a cape gooseberry (or a strip of
lemon zest) and enjoy.

SERVES 1

◇◇◇◇◇◇

TURMERIC WITH PASSION FRUIT

This refreshing cocktail is perfect enjoyed al fresco on a sultry summer's evening.

1½fl oz gin
1 tablespoon passion fruit and
   mango puree
1 tablespoon sugar syrup
1 tablespoon turmeric juice
   (see above)
squeeze of lemon juice
passion fruit and lime wedge,
   to garnish

Put the gin, passion fruit and mango puree, sugar syrup,
turmeric juice, and lemon juice in a cocktail shaker and
shake for about 20 seconds.

Strain into a glass full of ice, garnish with passion fruit
and a lime wedge, and enjoy.

BEAUTY

TURMERIC AND MILK FACE MASK

Due to its antibacterial, anti-inflammatory, and antioxidant properties, turmeric isn't just good for cooking with; it can be used as a beauty ingredient, too. The antiseptic and antibacterial properties are particularly beneficial for acne or blemish-prone skin, while the anti-inflammatory nature of turmeric makes it helpful for rosacea. It is important to use organic non-dyed turmeric for these recipes.

¼ cup rice flour

2 teaspoons organic ground turmeric

⅓ cup milk or yogurt

Mix all the ingredients together in a small bowl until well combined.

To use, cleanse your face and, while your skin is still a little damp, apply the mask to your face, avoiding the eye area. Relax and allow the mask to dry for about 5 minutes, then rinse off thoroughly with lukewarm water and pat your skin dry.

TURMERIC AND COCONUT OIL FACE MASK

Coconut oil, like turmeric, is known for its beauty-enhancing properties, so here is a mask combining both of these natural anti-aging ingredients.

½ tablespoon organic ground turmeric

1 tablespoon raw honey

3 tablespoons extra virgin coconut oil, melted

Mix all the ingredients together to make a paste. Apply to your (cleansed) face, avoiding the eye area, and relax for 10 minutes. Rinse off with lukewarm water and a clean facecloth. Pat your skin dry.

BODY SCRUB

This scrub is excellent for removing dead skin cells and gently exfoliating the skin, leaving it feeling a little more radiant and youthful.

½ tablespoon organic
   ground turmeric
¼ cup brown sugar
melted coconut oil

Mix the turmeric and sugar together and then add enough melted coconut oil, stirring, until you get the consistency of a body scrub.

In the shower, step aside from the water flow to apply the scrub to wet skin. Rub gently all over and then rinse off immediately in the shower.

INDEX

◇◇◇◇◇◇